poony 6/po 6-

D0880415

*Shroud
of the
Gnome*

ALSO BY JAMES TATE

Shroud
of the
Gnome

poems by

JAMES TATE

THE ECCO PRESS

THE ECCO PRESS
100 West Broad Street
Hopewell, New Jersey 08525

Published simultaneously in Canada by
Publishers Group West, Inc., Toronto, Ontario
Printed in the United States of America

Library of Congress Cataloging-in-Publication Data
Tate, James, 1943–
Shroud of the gnome : poems / by James Tate.—1ST Ecco ed.
p.   cm.
ISBN 0-88001-561-6.—ISBN 0-88001-562-4 (pbk)
I. Title.
PS3570.A8S55   1997
811'.54—dc21   97-16224

Designed by Susanna Gilbert, The Typeworks
The text of this book is set in Fairfield

9 8 7 6 5 4 3 2 1

FIRST PAPERBACK EDITION

for Dara

ACKNOWLEDGEMENTS

American Poetry Review, Boston Review, Boulevard, Colorado Review, Erewon, Field, Gettysburg Review, Grand Street, Green Mountain Review, Harvard Review, Iowa Review, Orbis, Partisan Review, Pequod, P. N. Magazine, Poets & Writers, Verse.

CONTENTS

"Here then, faintly discolored and liable to come apart if you touch it, is the corsage that I kept from the dance." —JAMES SALTER

Shroud
of the
Gnome

WHERE BABIES COME FROM

Many are from the Maldives,
southwest of India, and must begin
collecting shells almost immediately.
The larger ones may prefer coconuts.
Survivors move from island to island
hopping over one another and never
looking back. After the typhoons
have had their pick, and the birds of prey
have finished with theirs, the remaining few
must build boats, and in this, of course,
they can have no experience, they build
their boats of palm leaves and vines.
Once the work is completed, they lie down,
thoroughly exhausted and confused,
and a huge wave washes them out to sea.
And that is the last they see of one another.
In their dreams Mama and Papa
are standing on the shore
for what seems like an eternity,
and it is almost always the wrong shore.

DAYS OF PIE AND COFFEE

A motorist once said to me,
and this was in the country,
on a county lane, a motorist
slowed his vehicle as I was
walking my dear old collie,
Sithney, by the side of the road,
and the motorist came to a halt
mildly alarming both Sithney and myself,
not yet accustomed to automobiles,
and this particular motorist
sent a little spasm of fright up our spines,
which in turn panicked the driver a bit
and it seemed as if we were off to a bad start,
and that's when Sithney began to bark
and the man could not be heard, that is,
if he was speaking or trying to speak
because I was commanding Sithney to be silent,
though, indeed I was sympathetic
to his emotional excitement.
It was, as I recall, a day of prodigious beauty.
April 21, 1932—clouds,
like the inside of your head explained.
Bluebirds, too numerous to mention.
The clover calling you by name.
And fields oozing green.
And this motorist from nowhere
moving his lips

like the wings of a butterfly
and nothing coming out,
and Sithney silent now.
He was no longer looking at us,
but straight ahead
where his election was in doubt.
"That's a fine dog," he said.
"Collies are made in heaven."
"Well, if I were a voting man I'd vote for you," I said.
"A bedoozling day to be lost in the country, I say.
Leastways, I am a misplaced individual."
We introduced ourselves
and swapped a few stories.
He was a veteran and a salesman
who didn't believe in his product—
I've forgotten what it was—hair restorer,
parrot feed—and he enjoyed nothing more
than a day spent meandering the back roads
in his jalopy. I gave him directions
to the Denton farm, but I doubt
that he followed them, he didn't
seem to be listening, and it was getting late
and Sithney had an idea of his own
and I don't know why I am remembering this now,
just that he summed himself up by saying
"I've missed too many boats"
and all these years later

I keep thinking that was a man
who loved to miss boats,
but he didn't miss them that much.

They ask me if I've ever thought
about the end of the world,
and I say, "Come in, come in,
let me give you some lunch, for God's sake."
After a few bites it's the afterlife
they want to talk about. "Ouch," I say,
"did you see that grape leaf skeletonizer?"
Then they're talking about redemption
and the chosen few sitting right by His side.
"Doing what?" I ask. "Just sitting?"
I am surrounded by burned up zombies.
"Let's have some lemon chiffon pie
I bought yesterday at the 3 Dog Bakery."
But they want to talk about my soul.
I'm getting drowsy and see butterflies
everywhere. "Would you gentlemen
like to take a nap, I know I would."
They stand and back away from me,
out the door, walking toward my neighbors,
a black cloud over their heads
and they see nothing without end.

NEVER AGAIN THE SAME

Speaking of sunsets,
last night's was shocking.
I mean, sunsets aren't supposed to frighten you, are
    they?
Well, this one was terrifying.
People were screaming in the streets.
Sure, it was beautiful, but far too beautiful.
It wasn't natural.
One climax followed another and then another
until your knees went weak
and you couldn't breathe.
The colors were definitely not of this world,
peaches dripping opium,
pandemonium of tangerines,
inferno of irises,
Plutonian emeralds,
all swirling and churning, swabbing,
like it was playing with us,
like we were nothing,
as if our whole lives were a preparation for this,
this for which nothing could have prepared us
and for which we could not have been less prepared.
The mockery of it all stung us bitterly.
And when it was finally over
we whimpered and cried and howled.
And then the streetlights came on as always
and we looked into one another's eyes—

ancient caves with still pools
and those little transparent fish
who have never seen even one ray of light.
And the calm that returned to us
was not even our own.

After the burial
we returned to our units
and assumed our poses.
Our posture was the new posture
and not the old sick posture.
When we left our stations
it was just to prove we could,
not a serious departure
or a search for yet another beginning.
We were done with all that.
We were settled in, as they say,
though it might have been otherwise.
What a story!
After the burial we returned to our units
and here is where I am experiencing
that leg-kicking syndrome thing.
My leg, for no apparent reason,
flies around the room kicking stuff,
well, whatever is in its way,
like a screen or a watering can.
Those are just two examples
and indeed I could give many more.
I could construct a catalogue
of the things it kicks,
perhaps I will do that later.
We'll just have to see if it's really wanted.
Or I could do a little now

and then return to listing later.
It kicked the scrimshaw collection,
yes it did. It kicked the ocelot,
which was rude and uncalled for,
and yes hurtful. It kicked
the guacamole right out of its bowl,
which made for a grubby
and potentially dangerous workplace.
I was out testing the new speed bump
when it kicked the viscountess,
which she probably deserved,
and I was happy, needless to say,
to not be a witness.
The kicking subsided for a while,
nobody was keeping track of time
at that time so it is impossible
to fill out the forms accurately.
Suffice it to say we remained
at our units on constant alert.
And then it kicked over the little cow town
we had set up for punching and that sort of thing,
a covered wagon filled with cover girls.
But now it was kicked over
and we had a moment of silence,
but it was clear to me
that many of our minions
were getting tetchy

and some of them were getting tetchier.
And then it kicked a particularly treasured snuff box
which, legend has it, once belonged to somebody
named Bob Mackey, so we were understandably
saddened and returned to our units rather weary.
No one seemed to think I was in the least bit culpable.
It was my leg, of course, that was doing the actual
     kicking,
of that I am almost certain.
At any rate, we decided to bury it.
After the burial we returned to our units
and assumed our poses.
A little bit of time passed, not much,
and then John's leg started acting suspicious.
It looked like it wanted to kick the replica
of the White House we keep on hand
just for situations such as this.
And then, sure enough, it did.

THE BLIND HERON

Now Kiki's gone and lost her cockatiel, Lilith.
She's put signs up all over town offering a reward.
I don't hold out much hope for Lilith's return.
Given our New England climate she's probably
halfway to Australia by now. Kiki mopes around
feeling rejected, of course, taking it personally,
of course, as if Lilith were the final judge.
And it is true, Kiki has her problems: she's a liar,
for one thing, and not just your average prevaricator.
Kiki once arrived at a party at my house and announced
to everyone that "the President has just been shot."
We turned on the radio immediately, and it was true
the President had just been shot, but Kiki didn't
know this, it was her idea of an entrance,
or so we thought. But perhaps that was a poor example
of Kiki's essentially prevaricating nature.
Okay. One time I asked Kiki what she did over the
        weekend.
She said: "I went to Tasmania." That's nice, I said,
but please don't insult my credulity. Tasmania, hmmm.
What's the capitol of Tasmania? "Hobart," she said.
"I captured a very nice cockatiel while I was there.
Would you care to meet it?" Well, I met Lilith,
a nice looking bird, very nice, but I really don't think
Lilith is her real name. If I had flown to Tasmania
for the weekend and had captured a fine bird like that
I would have called her Christina the Astonishing,

I would have known beyond a doubt that that was her
    true name.
Why Kiki lies about such elementary truths is beyond
    me.
You can see why I considered it my duty to remove the
    bird
from Kiki's care, poor Kiki, and beautiful, glorious
Christina the Astonishing, who, by the way, is from
Australia, not Tasmania, of that I am almost certain.

ACTING ON A TIP

We went to the bug-eating state.
We sat down on some little bluestem grass.
Grasshoppers plague the state.
So who's eating the bugs?
Acting on a tip, we brushed our teeth.
This was going to be a very long drive.
Recumbent bison decorated the airwaves.
Acting on a tip, I got dressed and walked
down to the river and washed my face
and combed my hair and picked the bugs
from my teeth and urinated on a leaf.
The leaf was a moving target
as a crack squadron of soldier ants
had big plans for it elsewhere.
My yellow rain was meant to amuse them,
nothing more. What a glorious morning
for bugs in general, for caterpillars
speeding toward their destiny in the sky,
dragonflies mating in flight,
ancient beetles lugging their excess wisdom
to the auction block, and katydids
in charge of cryptography, and walking sticks
to remind us of how long the road can be.
And this is by no means an exhaustive catalogue.
One could prattle on about a variety of mites
until the cows come home. Instead,
let's talk about cows no more.

Acting on a tip, I zipped up
and returned to the beefsteak club in progress,
the raving, looting, windswept, boomeranging
family of vacationers to which I belong.
They were seated on a log discussing pork futures.
My beloved daughter Tabitha was breathing heavily.
There was a common earwig exiting her right ear,
or so I told her. "Daddy," she replied,
"that earwigs crawl into people's ears at night
and bite them is a totally unfounded superstition.
Earwigs are harmless, only occasionally damaging
flower blossoms." I scanned the horizon.
"Let's camp here," I said. "But Daddy,"
they announced in unison, "we *are* camped here."

And what amazes me is that none of our modern
     inventions
surprise or interest him, even a little. I tell him
it is time he got his booster shots, but then
I realize I have no power over him whatsoever.
He becomes increasingly light-footed until I lose sight
of him downtown between the federal building and
the post office. A registered nurse is taking her
coffee break. I myself needed a break, so I sat down
next to her at the counter. "Don't mind me," I said,
"I'm just a hungry little Gnostic in need of a sandwich."
(This old line of mine had met with great success
on any number of previous occasions.) I thought,
a deaf, dumb, and blind nurse, sounds ideal!
But then I remembered that some of the earliest
Paleolithic office workers also feigned blindness
when approached by nonoffice workers, so I paid my bill
and disappeared down an alley where I composed
     myself.
Amid the piles of outcast citizenry and burning barrels
of waste and rot, the plump rats darting freely,
the havoc of blown newspapers, lay the little shroud
of my lost friend: small and gray and threadbare,
windworn by the ages of scurrying hither and thither,
battered by the avalanches and private tornadoes

of just being a gnome, but surely there were good times,
    too.
And now, rejuvenated by the wind, the shroud moves
    forward,
hesitates, dances sideways, brushes my foot as if for a
    kiss,
and flies upward, whistling a little-known ballad
about the pitiful, raw etiquette of the underworld.

MY FELISBERTO

My felisberto is handsomer than your mergotroid,
although, admittedly, your mergotroid may be the wiser
    of the two.
Whereas your mergotroid never winces or quails,
my felisberto is a titan of inconsistencies.
For a night of wit and danger and temptation
my felisberto would be the obvious choice.
However, at dawn or dusk when serenity is desired
your mergotroid cannot be ignored.
Merely to sit near it in the garden
and watch the fabrications of the world swirl by,
the deep-sea's bathymetry wash your eyes,
not to mention the little fawns of the forest
and their flip-floppy gymnastics, ah, for this
and so much more your mergotroid is infinitely
    preferable.
But there is a place for darkness and obscurity
without which life can sometimes seem too much,
too frivolous and too profound simultaneously,
and that is when my felisberto is needed,
is longed for and loved, and then the sun can rise again.
The bee and the hummingbird drink of the world,
and your mergotroid elaborates the silent concert
that is always and always about to begin.

SAME AS YOU

I put my pants on one day at a time.
Then I hop around in circles hobbledehoy.
A projectile of some sort pokes me
in the eye—I think it's a bird
or a flying pyramid that resembles a bird.
Well it sure hurts and I'm swelling
even in areas where it's inappropriate
such as my cupola, also my cup of tea.
Flapdoodle is my middle name so I know
two specks about what's coming next:
the leopard's spots and their humorous sayings.
There are those who would suggest that
I am hog-tied and frequently late to work.
To which I reply: Indeed I am.
As a former ranchero and postmodern
farmerette I think we can speak freely
of the current crisis—the soil is creeping
out from under us and the haycocks
appear lubberly. If it's true
that you can judge a man's character
by the shape of his sandcastle,
then I say you are a squint-eyed stormy petrel,
and I a piebald crabstick,
which is like a dream come true.
We're practically carved out of the same carrot.
I for one can barely tell where I trail off
and you begin, since human beings are reported

to be ninety-eight percent duct tape
and feathers anyway. It's hard
to pull the pants on over all of this debris,
and once the greensward has been wrenched
into shape the going is so smooth
it's almost like not going at all.
Where have I been, where have I been?
Thus I was led into paths I had not known.

AT THE DAYS END MOTEL

I turned on the waterworks and said
"Well you don't need to make a federal case out of it."
But she did and I suppose she needed to.
Let's get out of this hellhole, I said.
That's a nice dog and pony show you have there, she
    said.
Be my guest, I said.
You're really chewing up the scenery tonight, she said.
And you, you're a predatory woman, one of easy morals,
    cheap and tawdry.
Hey listen schmendrick, at least I'm not an inept
    nonentity.
Aw, Cupcake, don't let's get cruel now, I can't help for
    stains on the wallpaper, okay?
You're like a rabbit responding very rapidly to food.
I confess, in a crutch and toothpick parade
    I would never single you out.

Down the road, about a quarter of a mile, a tractor trailer
    jackknifed and took a station wagon and a minibus
    with it straight to hell where they had some
    remarkably good carrot cake.
A jackal-headed god of the underworld
    joined them at their table
    and was surprisingly convivial.

Jim just loves to garden, yes he does.
He likes nothing better than to put on
his little overalls and his straw hat.
He says, "Let's go get those tools, Jim."
But then doubt begins to set in.
He says, "What is a garden, anyway?"
And thoughts about a "modernistic" garden
begin to trouble him, eat away at his resolve.
He stands in the driveway a long time.
"Horticulture is a groping in the dark
into the obscure and unfamiliar,
kneeling before a disinterested secret,
slapping it, punching it like a Chinese puzzle,
birdbrained, babbling gibberish, dig and
destroy, pull out and apply salt,
hoe and spray, before it spreads, burn roots,
where not desired, with gloved hands, poisonous,
the self-sacrifice of it, the self-love,
into the interior, thunderclap, excruciating,
through the nose, the earsplitting necrology
of it, the withering, shriveling,
the handy hose holder and Persian insect powder
and smut fungi, the enemies of the iris,
wireworms are worse than their parents,
there is no way out, flowers as big as heads,
pock-marked, disfigured, blinking insolently
at me, the me who so loves to garden

because it prevents the heaving of the ground
and the untimely death of porch furniture,
and dark, murky days in a large city
and the dream home under a permanent storm
is also a factor to keep in mind."

ACUPUNCTURE

Not the sleep of a baby, maybe,
but some sleep, a little sleep,
a few minutes here, a few minutes there,
it counts for something, not much,
some gold dust floating by, fool's gold,
and back in the dressing room, the reproach,
and the gallantry to go on,
and the body snatcher in the chest of drawers,
he too wanting a cigarette, hush,
the needle on the floor pestering
with its testimonials and revolutions,
the nonsense factor like sunshine in the face,
and the moth-eaten bookworm turning his pages
repeats the seven deadly sins but gets them
all wrong and curses, committing one.
But then it's silence that wakes you
with its huge beak and wings, its retching.
And the frog of a man you once knew
stares for hours down the throat of a nightingale.

SHUT UP AND EAT YOUR TOAD

The disorganization to which I currently belong
has skipped several meetings in a row
which is a pattern I find almost fatally attractive.
Down at headquarters there's a secretary
and a janitor who I shall call Suzie
and boy can she ever shoot straight.
She'll shoot you straight in the eye if you ask her to.
I mow the grass every other Saturday
and that's the day she polishes the trivets
whether they need it or not, I don't know
if there is a name for this kind of behavior,
hers or mine, but somebody once said something or
    another.
That's why I joined up in the first place,
so somebody could teach me a few useful phrases,
such as, "Good afternoon, my dear anal-retentive
    Doctor,"
and "My, that is a lovely dictionary you have on, Mrs.
    Smith."
Still, I hardly feel like functioning even on a brute
or loutish level. My plants think I'm one of them,
and they don't look so good themselves, or so
I tell them. I like to give them at least several
reasons to be annoyed with me, it's how they exercise
their skinny spectrum of emotions. Because.
That and cribbage. Often when I return from the club
late at night, weary-laden, weary-winged, washed out,

I can actually hear the nematodes working, sucking
the juices from the living cells of my narcissus.
I have mentioned this to Suzie on several occasions.
Each time she has backed away from me, panic-stricken,
when really I was just making a stab at conversation.
It is not my intention to alarm anyone, but dear Lord
if I find a dead man in the road and his eyes
are crawling with maggots, I refuse to say
have a nice day Suzie just because she's desperate
and her life is a runaway carriage rushing toward a cliff
now can I? Would you let her get away with that kind of
    crap?
Who are you anyway? And what kind of disorganization
    is this?
Baron of the Holy Grail? Well it's about time you got
    here.
I was worried, I was starting to fret.

He was never mean to me.
I never once heard him speak ill of another.
And he was always good by his word.
If he said he was bringing over a brace of quail
you set the table then and there.
Best of all, he was punctual,
a virtue I dearly love in a dog.
And he never crept, never crept, never crept.

NONSTOP

It seemed as if the enormous journey
was finally approaching its conclusion.
From the window of the train
the last trees were dissipating,
a childlike sailor waved once,
a seallike dog barked and died.
The conductor entered the lavatory
and was not seen again, although
his harmonica-playing was appreciated.
He was not without talent, some said.
A botanist with whom I had become acquainted
actually suggested we form a group or something.
I was looking for a familiar signpost
in his face, or a landmark that would
indicate the true colors of his tribe.
But, alas, there was not a glass of water
anywhere or even the remains of a trail.
I got a bewildered expression of my own
and slinked to the back of the car
where a nun started to tickle me.
She confided to me that it was her
cowboy pride that got her through. . . .
Through what? I thought, but drew my hand
close to my imaginary vest.
"That's a beautiful vest," she said,
as I began crawling down the aisle.
At last, I pressed my face against

the window: A little fog was licking
its chop, as was the stationmaster
licking something. We didn't stop.
We didn't appear to be arriving,
and yet we were almost out of landscape.
No creeks or rivers. Nothing
even remotely reminding one of a mound.
O mound! thou ain't around no more.
A heap of abstract geometrical symbols,
that's what it's coming to, I thought.
A nothing you could sink your teeth into.
"Relief's on the way," a little
know-nothing boy said to me.
"Imagine my surprise," I said
and reached out to muss his hair.
But he had no hair and it felt unlucky
touching his skull like that.
"Forget what I said," he said.
"What did you say?" I asked
in automatic compliance.
And then it got very dark and quiet.
I closed my eyes and dreamed of an emu I once loved.

Oftentimes, when the melancholy has gripped me,
the black bile has backed up into my craw,
the atrabilious cloud has settled over my head
and every last detail of life seems out of joint,
I tell myself it's time to visit Peter Bell,
my skewbald stallion. Combing his coat
brings a pleasure to us both it's safe to say,
time has no meaning for me, one animal
grooming another, and a wave at sea.
I read no thoughts into Peter Bell, simply
that he is happy enough with my quiet company.
We are both getting on in years now,
and while I know full well that regrets will get you
    nowhere,
how can I not from time to time remember
my dear wife Dorothy, not to mention her gooseberry pie,
and her Sunday dinners in general.
I try like hell not to become maudlin,
but being alone on a farm just isn't right.
The rooster crows, the sun comes up
and there's nothing but sick thoughts in my head.
I could shoot Peter Bell and move to town,
I wake with that thought nearly every morning.
Old Clyde would hire me on at the hardware store.
Rent a room from Matilda, drink
a couple of beers with the boys at The Green Parrot.
Too many mornings all that sounds like heaven to me.

DREAM ON

Some people go their whole lives
without ever writing a single poem.
Extraordinary people who don't hesitate
to cut somebody's heart or skull open.
They go to baseball games with the greatest of ease
and play a few rounds of golf as if it were nothing.
These same people stroll into a church
as if that were a natural part of life.
Investing money is second nature to them.
They contribute to political campaigns
that have absolutely no poetry in them
and promise none for the future.
They sit around the dinner table at night
and pretend as though nothing is missing.
Their children get caught shoplifting at the mall
and no one admits that it is poetry they are missing.
The family dog howls all night,
lonely and starving for more poetry in his life.
Why is it so difficult for them to see
that, without poetry, their lives are effluvial.
Sure, they have their banquets, their celebrations,
croquet, fox hunts, their seashores and sunsets,
their cocktails on the balcony, dog races,
and all that kissing and hugging, and don't
forget the good deeds, the charity work,
nursing the baby squirrels all through the night,
filling the birdfeeders all winter,

helping the stranger change her tire.
Still, there's that disagreeable exhalation
from decaying matter, subtle but ever present.
They walk around erect like champions.
They are smooth-spoken, urbane and witty.
When alone, rare occasion, they stare
into the mirror for hours, bewildered.
There was something they meant to say, but didn't:
"And if we put the statue of the rhinoceros
next to the tweezers, and walk around the room three
    times,
learn to yodel, shave our heads, call
our ancestors back from the dead—"
poetrywise it's still a bust, bankrupt.
You haven't scribbled a syllable of it.
You're a nowhere man misfiring
the very essence of your life, flustering
nothing from nothing and back again.
The hereafter may not last all that long.
Radiant childhood sweetheart,
secret code of everlasting joy and sorrow,
fanciful pen strokes beneath the eyelids:
all day, all night meditation, knot of hope,
kernel of desire, pure ordinariness of life,
seeking, through poetry, a benediction
or a bed to lie down on, to connect, reveal,
explore, to imbue meaning on the day's extravagant labor.

And yet it's cruel to expect too much.
It's a rare species of bird
that refuses to be categorized.
Its song is barely audible.
It is like a dragonfly in a dream—
here, then there, then here again,
low-flying amber-wing darting upward
and then out of sight.
And the dream has a pain in its heart
the wonders of which are manifold,
or so the story is told.

AND THAT'S THE GOOD NEWS

The man in the pharmacy yesterday
read the warning on the labels
on box after box of pills.
Each time his world crumbled
a little more and he reluctantly
returned the medicine
to its proper place on the shelf.
His nose was running,
his eyes leaked.
Every potential cure
had its attendant danger.
He was an advertisement
for despair. Finally
he just walked away.
His feet did a little dance
that meant nothing, and then
less than nothing, chicken scratches.
From a safe distance,
I followed him. We
had no idea where we were going.
We were like two ping-pong balls
floating, adrift
in a bathtub of black ink.

BEAUTIFUL NEW
MIRRORS HAVE ARRIVED

Of course that doesn't mean anything
by itself. You'd have to look into one
to be qualified, and even then your impressions
would be provisional, and I know you well enough—
parsimonious pepper pot—but who would want
that kind of temptation around the house,
there's work to do, there's so much stuff as it is
to pick up from the floor, polliwogs, firecrackers,
shrapnel of all kinds. And my studies, Retro-
gression and the Requiem Shark, to name but one area
I am immersed in, and there must be at least ten others,
so a beautiful new mirror is really out of the question.
And yet there is at least one part of me that would
like letting go, adios lifeboat, adieu palm-lined avenues,
old rabbit's foot you mean nothing to me now.
And what then? Oscillate through the underlife,
no projects, no deadlines, family or friends—
that's no way to travel, save for the dead
and they have little choice in the matter.
And, besides, I know what I look like,
I've caught glimpses of a hungry, stalking thing,
or a weak and wretched creature about to drop.
None of that interests me. A very funny sight
is a flamingo having its lunch upside down in the water.

Many queens were famous for their needlework.
You can do it at home, but I, for one, never do.
Flat, linked, buttonhole and knot stitches—
it can be a way of writing down history.
If a certain cow is sick, stitch a sick cow
and people will remember it. Or a loved one's
birthday, or a visit from the twins
on their new bicycles—hey, it's your needle.
Aprons, napkins, tablecloths, towels, potholders,
all these can be embroidered, and curtains, blouses.
But for the more ambitious needle jockey
the bedspread and the tapestry offer a more ample
    canvas.
Let us not forget the Bayeaux Tapestry, which shows
the Norman Conquest of England in the 11th century.
I wouldn't mock those of you who think
a border of pink tea roses perfect for a spread,
however I am inclined to favor visions—
ravens afire with emeralds for eyes,
vistas Magellan would shrink from,
smoke and fire and fog, addle-headed warthogs,
serpents that seem to go on forever,
secrets not to be fathomed,
a chaos of threads and colors,
vast dust clouds and flying horses,
balloon rides that last for centuries,
armies of assassins bedizened by hummingbirds,

or ululating housewives growing horns in the dark
    smocking—
a bedspread, in short, that insists you forget
everything else, rain on the rooftop and phone ringing,
that is embroidery of the highest power, strong
and inexhaustible and without rival.
I disremember that sick cow on the bicycle.

SCHOOL OF PADDLING

Piscatorially speaking,
we were out of luck.
We had traveled a great distance
and no one would speak to us
so we just sat there on the shore
and threw stones at stones
which led to the accidental erection
of a cairn, whose significance
we considered iffy at best.
Much later, after our departure,
warrior ants will clash by night,
or a great shrew will be buried there.
Or an important school of paddling
will spring up and the graduates
will be old and historic thanks
to us and our bad luck.
Joe opened a can of beans
and a falling star or a comet
grazed his shoulder,
or a firefly wanted to see
what kind of stuff we were made of;
then crawled back into his pocket for a smoke
and a free ride back to civilization—
which is to say, Jersey.

With all my knickknack injuries
and curiosity detours
and the embarrassing heartache
of my latest aperçu,
one would think I would have something
better to do than what I actually do
when I do what I actually do do.
I am always telling myself that
with no discernible effect as yet.
And yet I am always telling myself that.
It is a mystery to me, along with
so much better rubbish, even stylish rubbish,
the trash people are eager to kill for.
That's why I stay home, don't bother.
But I do bother, and it's not my home anyway.
I follow my thoughts around: they are
a constant torment to me, teasing me
as if I were some kind of schoolyard idiot.
Well, that seems appropriate, at least.

Excuse me, Mr. Odium-on-the-halfshell,
but there is a world out there
and it thinks precious little of you
and your suppurating, crinkled noggin.
I am bifurcating from you now.
I am on my own, a virginal spinster

on my way to joining some of the worldly clubs,
trend-setting organizations dedicated
to gorging themselves as well as replenishing
the harvest and saving humankind
from loutish ogres like yourself.
I am going to be out there on the front lines,
wherever they are, jousting with the issues,
contravening the inimical, cleaving
the stand-pat antipodes. O yes,
and I'm going to have a very good time
while doing all of this with a countenance
of unadulterated sunshine. So
here's hoping you rot in your cave,
Old Stick-in-the-Mud.
I stand by the kitchen window
for what seems like an eternity,
but in point of fact was probably thirty seconds.

Lover of stillness, lover of silence,
dreamer of small, fuzzy things,
king of the armchair cowboys,
I apologize for my fit of ill temper,
and, in truth, I have no grand plans.
(For a while there I thought I was going
to invade Holland—which was really scary.)
If you'll permit me, if you will be so kind,

I would like to stay right here with you,
maybe read the paper, catch up on the news,
and maybe later whip up some floating islands
of which we are both so inordinately fond.

THE FAULTS OF
THE MARINER'S COMPASS

He collects Bakelite from jerkwater towns like this,
and can shadow-dance on motel walls, vulpine
extravagances mostly, his Molly hasn't the stomach for,
although she can cut a mean lupine imitation
in a farmer's pasture fine enough to chase sheep
up a tree, so their relationship is complicated
and they seek counseling whenever they spot a shingle
offering some, even at the most ridiculous prices
and from people clearly wildered in their wits,
foaming at the mouth, etc. It's just part
of their road-routine and it seems to help.
Tom throws her a biscuit, she blows him a kiss,
and the miles roll by, and the woolgathering,
and the woolgathering, and the Bakelite gathering.
The pharmacy owner says, "Whatever would bring you
to our town? There's nothing here to see or do."
Clouds made in Heaven by the Master, a Chinaman
of immense whimsy. The lady in the bar at noon
says, "He makes me go to those damned dog races
every night. Why not a movie and dinner just once?"
Tom and Molly speeding alongside the coal trains
with a joy rarely afforded in a hospital or a bank.

IN HIS HUT SAT BABA JAGA,
HAG-FACED AND WITH A LEG OF CLAY

After the narrator's abrupt departure
several significant threads were left dangling
so, to break the tension, I chimed in:
What if a finger-sized peasant
makes off with a magic steed, eh?
(This seemed to please them.)
And Ivan eats a bird's giblets
which gives him the ability to spit up gold.
(Could feel my power growing.)
But this makes him very thirsty
and he drinks a great deal of beer.
Soon he is pixilated and experiences
an overwhelming desire to kiss his sister.
Ivan sets off on his quest.
Here, incidentally, also belongs the dialogue
between the stepmother and the chisel.
The sister, the homely Dorita,
dotes only on agrarian prosperity.

What would a mute be doing in a phone booth
at this hour, I asked myself. His lips seemed
to be blowing invisible bubbles, which were cute
until a red dragonfly crashed into them
and lost his way. An hour passed, but I felt
younger and pretty sure I would be getting
an important part in a movie, a man unable
to think of his name finds happiness in soup.
The mute is suddenly very angry and raising his voice
as if he had one. It appears that his girlfriend
has betrayed him in some fashion, perhaps
she met a soldier in an alley and they kissed.
But why would she tell him this, she could have
kept it a secret and he would never know, since,
I believe, the soldier shipped out that same evening.
And now the mute is sobbing, and this I can hear,
and it gets louder and louder until, finally,
I too am sobbing, it all seems so unfair.
It's almost midnight, and a million stars
drive slowly by in cars impossible to see.

"SODOMY IN SHAKESPEARE'S SONNETS"

The boy found himself lost in a misty forest.
No one he ever met failed to comment
on his peculiar heavenly odor.
He was finally rolled in broken pottery,
then locked up and left to starve.
He mailed his underwear back to his mother
who fled with them into the deep waters.

She's thinking, like a jaguar, or a dagger.
Words but more than words. Currents, hairpin
turns. It's scary but exciting. It's like dancing
on a precipice or sleeping under a waterfall.
She doesn't know the way home but she's running
and leaping over chasms in the earth, and she's singing
    too,
in a foreign language she's never heard spoken.
But the melody is one I've known all my life.
As a child I hummed it when I dreamed of her,
when I calculated the thousands of accidents it would
    take
to find her. And now her several rivers
are tossing up ancient maps with military strategies
traced in nearly invisible ink. She's typing, typing
in hot pursuit, a delirium possesses her,
she falls, gets up, shakes herself. A reverie
chases her through a forest, clippity clippity.
Then silence. Perhaps aphasia, or dysphasia.
She's a blind mystic who hasn't spoken in seven years.
She's walking backwards across a jumbo desert.
This is one of her more difficult passages.
A very obscure god peeks at her from the corner of a
    mirage.
And I think, that's my baby, come on baby,
you're in the homestretch now. But she won't

come home. She's hang gliding over a volcano
and has no use for the old ritual of "dinner."

FAULTY DICTION

My, but don't you look positively zodiacal today!
I shall maintain the stakeout for a while
if you would care to table-hop. I'm working
on a runic alphabet based on a secret discussion
I had yesterday with a paramilitary hot potato.
At least he was some kind of luminaria
in the Druze lumber business he insinuated.
He was also something of an expert in echolocation
so that when I dropped my comb he whistled
it back to me trippingly. Moussaka! I exclaimed.
Farkle, farkle, little star, he said with a smile.
I half expected him to vaporize right there, but
he didn't, and then he sort of did, at least
I didn't see him again. He was a nonparametric
nonsystem as far as I was concerned, in the grand
    manner.
Margaret, are you feeling alright? You're looking
a wee bit malarious. Perhaps you should try
hip-hopping about the tables, good for the circulation,
and I'll keep a watch out here for the malefactors
all the while ruminating rumbustiously on my new
runic alphabet, mellifluent memorandum whack whack.

God knows we've never thought of you
as insufficiently frou-frou.
I actually said that this morning
to my coffee, and the word recherché
was not far away, scowling at me.
I had a stranglehold on a straw man,
the son of a bitch was dying fast,
and then I let go and floated for a while.
Time passed like a butterfly in the room.
Suddenly I was in a bathtub, sinking.
And then I was on a couch for a long,
long time, and the butterfly landed
on me and held me in its scissors grip.
Page upon page of blank transcript.
A room inched sideways only slightly.
A nuthatch clung to the windowscreen.
Moments of great clarity inhabited me,
I was their anthill and they were my ants.
And they too must sleep, according to
a lot of prophets. And they will be
nameless, yes, and faceless, yes.
The prophets will boss them around
and insult their mothers, and the little ants
of clarity will just work harder and harder,
for they are blind and dedicated
and stupid, stupid, stupid.
This was revealed to me around 2:24 P.M., 9/27/95.

WHO WILL SEE ME THRU?

Not the morphodite from Oxnard
with the brilliant blue metallic luster
on the upper surface of his wings
and his thin veneer of stability,
he reminds me too much of my own mother,
which is another story altogether
and one that is not vaguely pertinent
to the chosen subject under consideration.
That would be a very different poem,
full of cunning and deluxe military strategy.
Sundry medieval torturing devices
would be employed to evoke my childhood days:
Ah, the joys of the strappado
and comfort of the rack.
Best of all, to be impaled!
Actual crucifixion was too good for me
she always said, that could wait
until I'd earned it.

As for that trollop who rebuffed me
on the school bus lo those many years ago,
never for one second have I forgotten
and have plotted my revenge day by day
across the rain puddles of the milky way.
That the virgin Dolly in pigtails
invited pinching is the unvarnished gospel.
I tell you now I am not criminally insane

and never once have I torched a great city.
But it is myself and myself alone
who suffered her contempt,
and I carry that wound like a birthright
and in this and in every other way
she is my mother's vile and abominable twin
who will see me thru, yes,
I said, who will see me thru.

Please don't taunt the scrivener
unless he's plopping around in a useless plot,
then you may lampoon him at will.
Don't butter the monkeys, just don't.
And no *etudes* on the ball field after eight.
Permits are required for flagellation,
keep your messianic woes to yourself.
Breathing on the bumblebees is strictly forbidden.
No muffins permitted in the aviary.
Talking dogs must keep it to a whisper.
Neither should you pee on the piglet.
You may boogie on the bridge but only lightly.
Try not to spend the summer in a state of torpor.
If you must eructate at the funeral
do so behind a bush, and make it sound
as if a rhinoceros is charging.
Do not write on the gazebo.
Do not sleep during the ranting.
Do not rant during the sleeping.
This is just a fragment of what I remember
of my childhood, and a roller coaster
I never dared ride, and some daisies,
and ghouls, thousands of ghouls
dancing on our graves. I mean rules,
thousands of rules digging our graves.
That's much better, that's approaching
the gazebo and deliberately, fiercely

writing on it, words that will cauterize
the delicate, the wan and sickly passerby:
Marcus Aurelius is a horse's ass.
There, now I can die with my boots on.

Hers was a docile parrot of few words
and fewer thoughts. It stared
at its little bit of seed
without recourse to self-pity,
though it would not have been inappropriate
to cry a little. The evening suggested
everyone could have made better plans.
The street lamps came on and a child
ducked into a doorway.
Mademoiselle de Boeff was powdering
her bosom. Some of the powder fell
onto her parrot. "Alas, it is snowing!"
it shrieked, and, with that, they both retired.

Some days I stand by the window
and watch the birds flit between
bush and tree and bird feeder
until my thoughts are fewer and fewer.
Glassy-eyed, the letters I should write
are forgotten bits of scenery.
"Dear Mr. Junco, the grey suit you wear today
has washed all my cares away."
I barely notice that blood is seeping
through the walls of my fortress.
I pray that pilgrims ignore
my site-specific installation.
I am an alien twig tossed in the corner,
a blot of faint rain
waiting for the right occasion.
I am hoping that a nuthatch will alight
on my wrist, and there will be a little message
neatly tied to its leg.
Great events: eggs hatching, trains
crashing, flowers unfolding,
lovers hopping about, dogs diving
from balconies, children somersaulting
in clover, and I am invited,
I can go if I want to, I am even a part
of the scene so much more
than I care to admit. I am *central,*

a focal point in the drama.
So much for being pushed around
by the tidal forces of history.
I will do my best to provide
a beacon of hope to those less fortunate
than myself. I shall remain modest
but dignified. And now
I really must get some sleep.
Tomorrow, the world!

SMART

I had a theory for a while,
but I had to let it go.
It was wasting away in captivity.
It sat there in the cage of my brain
and wouldn't eat.
When I had first trapped it
it was beautiful and wild and amused everyone.
"Too much attention," the vet said.
It wasn't cut out for that kind of life.
But when I tried to imagine
letting it go back to the craggy, brambly,
uproarious and vehement landscape
of its origin, I realized
I had sucked its lifeblood from it.
It stood no chance
of survival against those beasts
never glimpsed by man,
never photographed,
never tagged,
spooks with pigtails
lumbering through love songs
in lunatic lunchrooms,
and then dueling with cowboy snowbirds.
My little nothing had forgotten its tricks.
So I let it loose in a city park
whereupon a desperate pensioner

immediately recognized it
as the golden goose
or some such rubbish.

THE SLEEPING DISORDER TOUR

She would awake in the middle of the night
to tell me that we were in Nebraska,
or that we would be in Nebraska soon,
or that Nebraska was chasing us
and was trying to annex us and wanted
to question us down at police headquarters.
Then she'd drift away, wheezing fitfully,
and I'd lie there keeping watch over the herds,
chatting with Andrew Drips of the Missouri Fur
    Company.
"This place is uninhabitable," I told him.
"And wholly unfit for cultivation," he added.
I stared at the ceiling. Time itself
was a prairie schooner bumping and rolling
across the Great Plains in no big rush
to meet the surprises it was bound to meet.
Then I'd fall off, unawares, into a shallow rut,
and she'd rise up singing "Beautiful Nebraska!"

Even the abandoned husk of a person can sometimes
perform useful tasks and enjoy mildly good times,
light opera, dusting for cobwebs with long brooms, etc.
We walk a little, pause, look down, walk.
It's not a big effort to do any of this.
It's not as though we were crossing the forbidden
territory of Lop against icy gales,
but we would like to know what is on our minds—
a maze?—when we organize these shadows—
a slumber party?—so seductively, and yet
    incomprehensibly,
until we can't find ourselves anymore,
those selves that have been following us
and pestering us all these years,
which is not necessarily a bad thing.
Oh you talk a good game, Binky. I can see
that you have a nervous system shaped like Florida.
A lot of good that will do you when it's time
to trace your steps back into the egg.
Did I say egg? I meant dog.
If there are no secrets to be revealed
then I shall resume darning my other sock.
And if there are they best be espied
over at Binky's place, his rotunda has a view of some.
And then when we walk back it won't follow us.
We won't even remember its name

but our next big tag sale will be ablaze with bargain
    incubators.
And that's all I asked for was a clue.

At the intersection, cool as a moose,
stood a supernatural being,
and I waved but did not honk.
He or she was no cosmic bum,
but delicate and well grouped.
A great eschatological ferment
was at work. Ah, there's Lavinia
draped over a parking meter,
though she's not for sale,
she told me that herself.
And there's Orc with his face
like a pincushion. He still lives
in the Carboniferous Period.
And there are three hominids
entering Antonio's Pizza.
They are tiny and will have to stand
on one another's shoulders
to be noticed at all.
And the invertebrates themselves
are back in town
asking to be counted.
A great eschatological ferment, yes.
On my way to a very ancient shrine
and thinking about Cleopatra's nose
had it been shorter.
Most of these people have big plans,
careers the likes of which

I can barely imagine.
Cop a plea, cop a nod, that kind of thing.
Can't wait to go to the cold-meat party.
Little boyo saying, *Pass the buddha, please.*

I LEFT MY COUCH IN TATAMAGOUCHE

I desired lemonade—
It was hot and I had been walking for hours—
but after much wrestling,
pushing and shoving,
I simply could not get my couch
through the restaurant door.
Several customers and the owner
and the owner's son
were kinder than they should have been,
but finally it was time to close
and I urged them to return to their homes,
their families needed them
(the question of who needs what
was hardly my field of expertise).
That night, while sleeping peacefully
outside the train station
on my little, green couch,
I met a giantess by the name of Anna Swan.
She knelt beside my couch
and stroked my brow with tenderness.
She was like a mother to me
for a few moments there under the night sky.
In the morning, I left my couch in Tatamagouche,
and that has made a big difference.

TWENTY-FIVE

Twenty-five is such a big number
if you're talking about how many times I make love every
    day.
But if that's all the years she lived,
although she was a full-time nudist
and necromancer, it seems so insignificant
and one might even say "Why bother?"
Only twenty-five soldiers showed up
on the day the war was supposed to start
and everyone agreed it wasn't worth bothering with.
Refreshments were served, and no one mentioned
the number twenty-five for a while.
And this too is barely worth mentioning:
time passed, but no one knew just how much.
It felt like just a little bit,
although several very young people disagreed.
"This must be the beginning of the end," said an old one,
which turned out to be a cliché everyone loved.
At lunch, next door to the embassy, Philip announced:
"I'm sick of his clichés. Each time we approach
a genuine breakthrough in understanding he says
something like 'This must be the beginning of the end.'"
Twenty-five minutes later, he was sleeping like a baby,
which I realize is a cliché and I only say it
to punish him, to torment him so that he might in fact
stop "sleeping like a baby" if he so hates clichés.
Sleep like an improper integral, I say.

Sleep like a permutation group.
Perhaps it is still high-tea time where you reside.
If so, I pity you.
Some things are just not worth getting senile about.
I can't think of one right off, but give me a little time.
I'm in the middle of something,
or what I'm trying to say is
congratulations on staying alive.

BRAVE FACE

It seemed as if, for as long as we could remember,
evil days and hard times stalked us,
singled out the weak and the strong as well.
The beautiful and the good were shown no mercy.
And all the while we believed in a better day.

We sang the songs of praise and the songs of parting.
And at those gatherings, when food was prepared
in celebration, a wolf circulated
in the spirit world where only his whims mattered.
Not nice to admit it, but one ached for normalcy.

To enjoy what was left, one would be considered
a traitor to the cause, and this increasingly
angered me. I eventually confided in my wife
half expecting her to throttle me on the spot.
And that is precisely what she did.

And then we made sweet love and watched the sunset.
"What you are feeling is not different than the rest,"
she said. (I was feeling her breast at the time
and the rest were not.) A story like this
doesn't really end. A wolf goes from door to door

through all the streets of the village.
It pauses here and there, but we do not know

what it thinks, or if it thinks at all.
Laughter, of almost any kind, seems to frighten it.
That and the sound of its own name.

Think of your absent friend—
and I say, pig iron!
The bumbershoot has departed for the desert
using the back staircase and through the backdoor
incognito hush-hush catlike like a cloud
and what's a friend going to do
but cleave and cling, remembering
the flying horse, the chained maiden, Berenice's hair,
not to mention foreign bodies in the eye,
convulsions and loss of limb,
in addition to forms of address for persons of rank
and public office, and the Republic of Tonga!
I think of my absent friend
and all of this and so much more
whistles through my nervous system—
snowy tree crickets, toothpick grasshoppers,
immunization schedules for children,
golden parachutes, seasonal adjustments,
my friend, the last gasp of an old regime,
my friend, apogee of Central Asian Power,
my friend in the home of Knute Rockne
and who knows the living arrangements of young adults
    all too well,
not to mention most of the injuries and illnesses in
    industry,
absent now and gone
like the cholera epidemic in Peru is now gone, history,

and even as the jobless rate continues to rise,
so my friend is absent, is a nonpresence,
and is everywhere reminding me.

The new ergonomics were delivered
just before lunchtime
so we ignored them.
Without revealing the particulars
let me just say that
lunch was most satisfying.
Jack and Roberta went with
the corned beef for a change.
Jack believes in alien abduction
and Roberta does not,
although she has had
several lost weekends lately
and one or two unexplained scars
on her buttocks. I thought
I recognized someone
from my childhood
at a table across the room,
the same teeth, the same hair,
but when he stood up,
I wasn't sure, Squid with a red tie?
Impossible. I finished
my quiche lorraine
and returned my thoughts
to Jack's new jag:
"Well, I guess anything's
possible. People disappear
all the time, and most of them

have no explanation
when and if they return.
Look at Tony's daughter
and she's never been the same."
Jack was looking as if
he'd bet on the right horse now.
"And these new ergonomics,
who really designed them?
Does anybody know?
Do they tell us anything?
A name, an address? Hell no."
Squid was paying his bill
in a standard-issue blue blazer.
He looked across the room at me
several times. He looked tired,
like he wanted to sleep for a long time
in a barn somewhere, in Kansas.
I wanted to sleep there, too.

PER DIEM

Spherically wondrous sunbeam
dwelling in the mansion
of the pine of chastity,
today we bought an ice pack
for Mildred's injured foot.
Luminous shadow
in the plumflower chamber,
Edna quit her job yesterday,
got drunk, stayed drunk,
behaved like a defective monster
collapsing in the mansion
of self-pity. Meanwhile,
the great sea of compassion
rolled in, rolled out, rolled in.
And the blue mountain
of itself remains,
and the blind shampooers
never tire of their work.

ABOUT THE AUTHOR

JAMES TATE won the Pulitzer Prize and the William Carlos Williams Award in 1992 for his *Selected Poems* and the National Book Award for his 1994 collection, *Worshipful Company of Fletchers.* In 1995 the Academy of American Poets awarded him the Tanning Prize. Tate teaches at the University of Massachusetts in Amherst. *Shroud of the Gnome* is his twelfth collection.